Gary Jones

Edinburgh

Contents

1

Introduction

Thank you for downloading the book "Edinburgh Travel Guide"

This book contains information about the charming city of Edinburgh, which is located in Scotland's Central Belt. This book will help you enjoy the unique attractions it has to offer. From castles steeped with a rich history to modern art galleries showcasing Scotland's high cultural society, the town is a serendipitous adventure waiting to happen.

Hailed as one of the most beautiful cities in Europe, Edinburgh is a town, which combines idyllic historical landmarks with the exciting and bustling cityscape environment. With so much to offer, it is Scotland's not so secret and widely popular holiday destination.

This guide features chapters dedicated to giving you all the information you need to have a splendid holiday in Scotland's capital city. Below are the chapters included in this book:

- About Edinburgh: A Brief History and Background
- Geographical and Weather Information
- The Best Time to Go: Holiday and Tourist Dates
- Top 5 Places to Stay at on a Budget
- Famous Landmarks That Shouldn't be Missed
- Getting Around: Edinburgh Transportation
- The Art Scene: Museums and Galleries to See
- The Gastronomic Scene: Restaurants and Coffee Shops
- Edinburg Night Life

- The Whiskey Experience
- Only in Edinburgh: What You Can Only Experience in Edinburgh
- Staying Safe While on Holiday
- Recommended 3 Day Travel Itinerary

Thank you again for downloading the book and let's get started on exploring this beautiful city!

2

About Edinburgh: A Brief History and Background

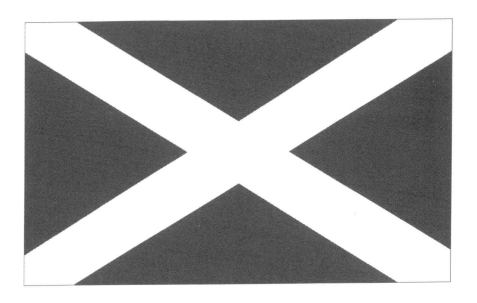

Edinburgh lies at the Central Belt, right in between the Highlands and the Southern Uplands. It is the capital of Scotland and has been that since the 15th century. It is the seat of monarchy and houses the Scottish Parliament.

It is the second most populous city in the country and the 7th in all of the United Kingdom. With such a large population, it is easy to see how it could be a place of diverse activities.

The earliest settlement in Edinburgh can be traced as far back as the 15th century, but before that, it was a fort. However, archeological proof of earlier inhabitants shows that there were already people living in the area as early as the Mesolithic Era.

The volcanic plug, more popularly known as Castle Rock, which sits in the middle of Edinburgh, served as a strategic and effective site for a fort. Rising an impressive 130 meters above sea level, it was a position that could easily be defended. When the English captured this part of Scotland in the 7th century, it was called Eiden's Burg. The term burg is an older word for fort and was added to "Eiden", which was what the area was called.

After serving as a fort, Edinburgh became home to Augustinian and Dominican Friars who both preached and helped commerce to improve. The town grew until it earned a chapter, which gave the residents certain rights. With its growing importance, the town once again fell under the English rule. The succeeding years witnessed the continuous warfare between England and Scotland with Edinburgh being caught in the middle.

By the 15th century, despite the continuous alternating invasions from Scotland and England, Edinburgh's population had grown to 15,000. The following centuries proved to be quite eventful with tragedies, such as the plague in the 17th and 19th centuries. There were also glorious occasions like the coronation of Charles I and the continuous improvement of the cityscape.

By the mid 19th century, Edinburgh had more than 170,000 residents. With the railway reaching the town and bridges built to provide more access, more and more immigrants made the Scottish town their new homes.

With such a long and rich history, Edinburgh has been home to distinguished experts in diverse fields, such as architecture, the arts, and sciences. Below are some of the famous folks who came from this town.

Alexander Graham Bell – Born in 1847, this Edinburgh native is the scientist, inventor, and engineer who has been credited in getting the patent for the first practical telephone.

Charles Darwin – Dubbed as the Father of Evolution, Darwin briefly called Edinburgh home when he attended the University of Edinburgh, which was then the best medical school in the United Kingdom. He stayed at the University from 1825–1827.

Sir Arthur Conan Doyle – This world famous literary writer was born in Edinburgh in 1859. He is the celebrated creator of Sherlock Holmes, a gifted detective with extraordinary sleuthing skills. With the popularity of his novels, this Edinburgh native is known to readers of all ages all over the world.

Sean Connery – Born in 1930, this Scottish actor has relished in the limelight. He was the first actor to portray the dashing British spy, James Bond, on the big screen. His other notable movies include Indian Jones, The Hunt for Red October and The Rock. His many awards and recognitions include the Kennedy Center Honors in 1999 and a knighthood in July of 2000 from Elizabeth II.

3

Geographical and Weather Information

Edinburgh lies on the Southern shore of the Firth of Forth, with the city center about 2 ½ miles from southwest of the Leith shoreline. The modern city is built on seven hills reminiscent of Rome's geography. The hills were products of ancient volcanic activity or intensive glaciations.

These hills are the following:
- Castle Rock
- Arthur's Seat
- Calton Hill
- Corstorphine Hill
- Craiglockhart Hill
- Braid Hill

- Blackford Hill

While the city is progressive with expansions regularly on the way, it is encircled by a green belt, which greatly affects the way it is developed. A green belt is an area protected from urban development to preserve it for natural wildlife. Expansions made in these areas must follow strict policies to ensure that these do not negatively affect the land. This is one of the many reasons why Edinburgh stayed lush despite being a cosmopolitan city.

Edinburgh is made up of different districts and areas, much like any other populated city. These areas retain the characteristics of the early settlements that were already in existence since the middle ages.

Residence types vary depending on the location. The ones located in the central part of the city are buildings with multiple occupants who are commonly known as "tenements". Residences on the Southern and Western parts of the city are mostly detached or semi-detached villas as these areas have traditionally been the more affluent ones.

One other interesting part of Edinburgh is the Old and New Towns. UNESCO declared these areas as World Heritage Sites in 1955.

Edinburgh, much like the rest of Scotland, has a temperate maritime climate. This often comes as a surprise to most visitors, as it is not as cold as one usually expects from a city located that far north. Daytime winter temperature rarely falls below freezing point while summer months are also mild, not often exceeding 22 degrees Celsius.

Its location between the coast and the hills has earned the city the nickname the windy city. With winds coming from the southwestern and eastern direction, rain and fog have become the norm in Edinburgh.

4

The Best Time to Go: Holiday and Tourist Dates

With its mild and friendly climate, Edinburgh is a year-long destination, which both the locals and the foreign tourists can fully enjoy.
However, to get a full experience of what the city has to offer, here are

the best times to come and enjoy the local life.

Summer

This is undeniably the best time to be in Edinburgh. The months of June, July and August are full of activities and local events that are sure to give you a more memorable stay. With the warm, pleasant weather, you can enjoy the charming and vibrant city and experience the world's largest art festival.

The Edinburgh Festival runs from the end of July to the beginning of September. The Festival has about ten different events packed within the few weeks of summer. The following are just some of the most popular events included in the celebration:

Edinburgh Festival Fringe –

More locally referred to as the "Fringe", this festival is one of the events that draw crowds to this idyllic and cosmopolitan city. The festival's name may have been influenced by the fact that experimental and challenging performances are often included in the programs. These types of performances are often not invited to participate in more traditional art festivals.

In 2015, the Fringe lasted for 25 days with more than 50,000 performances and over 3,000 shows in 313 venues all over the capital.

The Fringe is an open-access festival, which means everyone can participate in the different categories including theater, comedy, opera, dance and a lot more. It is a festival, which helped build the careers of different artists and turned aspiring individuals into household names.

Edinburgh is a cultural haven during the Fringe, with events happening in various venues. Performances take place all over the city – from conventional halls and stadiums to the back of a taxi cab. By simply walking down the street, you can view art shows on sidewalks, watch a musical in the corner and perhaps listen to a band playing some awesome music for passers-by.

The different events range from paid performances to free ones where you simply donate what you please at the end of the show. The Fringe turns the city into a paradise for art lovers of all shapes and sizes.

Edinburgh International Festival –
This is an annual festival, which runs for three weeks in August. Performances for this one are strictly by invitation of the Festival Director. This gathers top performers in performance, music and

other forms of art and serves to enrich the cultural life of Scotland, the UK, and Europe. The festival was first held after the Second World War as a way to bring back the arts into a war-torn Europe.

Edinburgh was chosen to host it as it fits the criteria organizers were looking for. They needed a city, which is capable of handling the large crowds that would be taking part or watching the performances. However, it had to be as picturesque as the cities that had previously hosted other similar festivals pre-war.

Other cities in the United Kingdom were considered before Edinburgh was eventually chosen. The festival performances are held in seven prominent venues located all over the city, including The Edinburgh Playhouse, Usher Hall, and Festival Theater. The 2016 festival included classical and contemporary performances of music, theater, dance, opera and workshops. Being in Edinburgh at the time of the festival will be a cultural experience that you will never forget.

Royal Edinburgh Military Tattoo −

A tattoo is a musical display or performance done by the military. This military tattoo is performed by the British Armed Forces, Commonwealth and other military bands. It is performed right in the heart of the city in front of the Edinburgh Castle.

The event draws thousands of people to Edinburgh to witness the spectacular performance. Two-thirds of the folks who come to see the tattoo are made up of local tourists with the rest coming from all over the world.

The popular military tattoo has sold out in advance for the past decade with people wanting to come and enjoy the musical performance done by the military personnel. To ensure that more folks get to enjoy the tattoo and hype up a little bit more excitement, the military bands also do free abridged performances in the Princes' Street Gardens. The musical performance is dubbed as "Taste of the Tattoo."

The mini-show allows those who purchased tickets to the main performance to still enjoy the tattoo. In addition, it provides those who will be watching the Edinburgh Castle performance a preview of what the bands have in store for them.

Spectators are treated to a different side of the military with these entertaining musical performances of an artistic display of military precision.

Military Tattoo Website

http://www.edintattoo.co.uk/

Edinburgh International Book Festival or EIBF –

This event happens on the last three weeks of August and is held at the center of the Scottish capital at the Charlotte Square. It is the world's largest book festival, which draws book lovers of all ages from the four corners of the globe.

From the first time it was held in 1983, the book festival has brought to Edinburgh thousands of authors and publishers to share their love for literature with excited fans. Authors and personalities who have been a part of the festival include Margaret Atwood, Al Gore, Ian Rankin and Harry Potter creator, JK Rowling.

The EIBF is a festival designed for adults and kids alike. The Children's program runs alongside the general one and provides the youngsters with various activities, such as storytelling, workshops, and author events.

So if you or your traveling companions are book lovers, then this is the perfect time to spend a few weeks in the beautiful city.

International Edinburg Film Festival or EIFF –

First opening its gates in 1947, the EIFF is the oldest running film festival in the world. The event features a range of shows from full-length films to documentaries and music videos. It also recognizes top class entries with distinguished awards. These awards include the Michael Power award given by the jury and Audience Award going to crowd favorites.

The Edinburgh Filmhouse serves as the festival's home, with the featured films and videos shown in various venues all over the city. The EIFF segregate the entries into different categories that include, but are not limited to, animation, short films, and special screenings. So whatever genre you are interested in, you will find something to enjoy during the EIFF.

Autumn

With the festivals coming to an exciting close at the beginning of this season and the whole city turning a golden shade, Fall is a spectacular time to be roaming the streets of Edinburgh. There is still one more festival though that is an autumnal tradition, the International Storytelling Festival. So, if you are in town, then go ahead and check out the story telling events that are happening, featuring both traditional and contemporary.

Autumn is also when Bonfire Night happens. This amazing evening highlighted by an entertainment program and a half-hour fireworks show is also more popularly known locally as Guy Fawkes Night.

However, if you are more of a nature person, a walk around the city is a feast for your eyes. Edinburgh's 112 parks turn into a kaleidoscope of warm earth colors. The gorgeous palette of hues combined with the warm weather creates a relaxing environment. So, whether you go for a stroll down the historical streets or enjoy a cup of coffee in one of the local cafés, autumn in Edinburgh is a getaway worth taking.

Winter

The winter months in Edinburgh are truly a merry time. Christmas celebrations and Hogmanay draw hundreds of tourists to the city to take part in the festivities. In typical Edinburgh fashion, the celebrations last for weeks. The Christmas Season kicks off on November 18 and for six whole weeks, the entire city buzzes with excitement.

Kids of all ages will have a blast with the two ice skating rinks that are put up to help everybody get into the holiday spirit. What is winter after all if not for those afternoons spent gliding along the ice under a sprinkle of falling snow. So whether you and your family choose the ring-shaped rink St. Andrew's Square or the more traditional one Princes Street Gardens, you are guaranteed to have hours of fun and laughter.

One other thing that you and your traveling companions should certainly not miss is an afternoon spent exploring the Christmas Markets. This is perfect for you if you are looking for last minute gifts or souvenirs or just simply want to have the most Christmassy experience outside the North Pole. With fairy lights lining the street and the smell of bratwurst wafting from the shops, you will definitely find yourself humming a Christmas carol as you stroll up and down the streets.

Being in town during the winter season also means you get a chance to be part of the Hogmanay celebrations. Hogmanay is the Scottish word used to refer to the last day of the year, so the celebration is literally a New Year's Eve party, but this one is by no means a simple one. The evening kicks off with streets bursting on the seams with revelers. Concerts and other performances are the norm as people wait for the highlight of the evening, which is, of course, the fireworks display at midnight.

You can choose to take part in the Torchlight Procession, which leads up to Calton Hill. It's remarkable finale of fire lighting, and fireworks are sure to be an experience you will remember for years to come.

Spring

This season is probably the quietest time to be in the city. If you are looking for a more relaxing holiday away from the crowds, then head on to Edinburgh during the months of spring. While not busy, the city is glorious at this time with the parks in vibrant colors from the flowers blooming in all their glory.

If you will be traveling with children, spring is also a good time to head on to the picturesque city. The International Science Festival and Imaginate Festival take place during this season.

The Edinburgh International Science Festival takes place either in March or April. It is a 2-week discovery of how science and technology can improve the way of life. It draws both adults and kids alike to the city, as they take part in a varied program including talks, exhibits and fun-filled family days.

The Imaginate Festival in Edinburgh happens towards the end of spring and is one dedicated to little kids. It features some of the best performances and theater and dance that are guaranteed to keep your little ones entertained.

Whatever season you decide to head on over to the Scottish capital, you will certainly find something to enjoy. This is perhaps the reason why thousands of tourists decide to enjoy holiday in the city, which fuses the excitement of city living with the enchantment of being close to nature.

5

The Top 5 Places to Stay at on a Budget

With so many things happening in Edinburgh all year round, one of the most challenging things you will probably experience is finding a place to stay. The great news is that there are different types of accommodations available all around the city.

While like any other capital city, it has its fair share of 5-star hotels and resorts it may not be the most cost-efficient way to enjoy your holiday. Other options available are budget hotels or holiday inns, contemporary hotels with warm Scottish ambiance and small elegant boutiques. This wide range of options means you can find what fits your budget without compromising comfort.

Here are some of the best places to stay at where you can get value for your money:

Rock House –

Nestled on the slopes of Calton Hill, this immaculate 18th-century house is one of the most recommended places to stay at when visiting Edinburgh. While only accessible by foot, it is only a few minute walk away from famous Princes Street. It is perfect for visitors who want to experience the city but who prefer to stay away from a conventional hotel setting.

Spectacular views of the city can be seen from virtually any part of the house. With delightfully remodeled rooms, the historic house offers comfortable amenities such as free Wi-Fi to keep you and your family happy. If you plan to stay for the day, then you can relax in the courtyard or walled gardens for an afternoon of peace and quiet.

One other appealing feature about the Rock House is its friendly prices. Room rates range from £60 - £150 a day with better prices offered for a longer stay.

Address:28 Calton Hill, Edinburgh EH7 5AA
Phone:0131 558 1108
Rock House Website
http://rockhouse-edinburgh.com/
Rock House Map
https://goo.gl/maps/Q4TeA9SrHSN2

Old Waverly Hotel –

This is Edinburgh's oldest and most famous hotel located on Princes Street. The historical hotel is still one of the best accommodation options for visitors of the Scottish Capital. It is ideal for both tourists and corporate guests as it is close to the Financial District, as well as to some of the popular attractions in the city.

With affordable rooms that offer a spectacular view of the famous Princes Street, the Old Waverly Hotel remains a favorite all year round. The hotel also offers amazing deals, such as their winter £1 offer where guests only pay a pound per person per night. One other attraction that the hotel offers is it's in house restaurant "Cranston's Restaurant". The menu features local and traditional Scottish cuisine, which is an experience one should not miss when visiting Edinburgh.

Address:43 Princes St, Edinburgh
Phone:0131 556 4648
Old Waverly Hotel Website
http://www.oldwaverley.co.uk/
Old Waverly Hotel Map
https://goo.gl/maps/QrTqFRgnXzG2

Ten Hill Place Hotel –

This Eco-Friendly award winning hotel is located in Old Town, away from the main city traffic. However, it is still close to the Festival Theater and University of Edinburgh, which makes it a popular choice of tourists coming into the capital for the Edinburgh Festival. The hotel has a sophisticated ambiance, making it a preferred place to stay at for conferences or business trips.

Ten Hill Place has spacious rooms that offer good value for your money with complete amenities, such as WI-FI. It also boasts of friendly staff ready who are to help you out – from giving directions to the nearest Edinburgh attraction to ensuring you have a comfortable night. With affordable rooms and appealing packages offered, it is no wonder this hotel has gotten rave reviews from guests.

Address:10 Hill Pl, Edinburgh
Phone:0131 662 2080
Ten Hill Place Hotel Website
https://www.tenhillplace.com/
Ten Hill Place Hotel Map
https://goo.gl/maps/8sDCvVQWCP72

Brooks Hotel −

This newly refurbished boutique hotel located at the west end of the city center has been raking in great reviews from satisfied guests. The beautiful architecture and friendly ambiance has had a positive impact to those who chose to stay at the Brooks Hotel.

Located close to public transportation, the hotel has become a favorite stylish place to stay at for visitors who want to explore and experience the amazing Scottish capital. With prices ranging from £59 to £99, the spacious rooms with comfortable beds and power showers give you absolute value for your money.

Address:70-72 Grove St, Edinburgh
Phone:0131 228 2323
Brooks Hotel Website
http://www.brooksedinburgh.com/
Brooks Hotel Map
https://goo.gl/maps/tmGSzWnsJXU2

Fountain Court Apartments-Morrison −

One other accommodation option that visitors to Edinburgh can choose are serviced apartments. These have grown quite popular in the last few years as more and more tourists opt to stay away from impersonal hotel rooms. They prefer their own spaces where it feels like home and they can prepare their own meals if they want to.

Fountain Court Apartments offer this option at affordable prices. With prices ranging from £79 to £89, accommodations will certainly fit your budget. These pet friendly apartments also come with basic amenities, such as WI-FI access, kitchen and laundry facilities.

Address:228 Morrison St, Edinburgh
Phone:0131 622 6677
Fountain Court Apartments-Morrison Website
http://www.fountaincourtapartments.com/
apartments/morrison/
Fountain Court Apartments-Morrison Map
https://goo.gl/maps/oVpGztfPRdm

6

Getting Around: Edinburgh Transportation

Getting around the city is quite easy and manageable with attractions located close to each other. With other sites that are a bit further away, public transportation is available all throughout the city. Below are the different ways to get around the Scottish capital:

Trams –

Opened in 2014, the Tram line operates between the Airport and the city center. It passes through Princes Street, Haymart, Murrayfield Stadium, the Stenhouse Area and Gyle. Tram fees are the same as the Lothian bus fares. One other great thing about this public transportation is that you can use Lothian Day Tickets and Ridacards to pay for fare.

Phone:0131 475 0177
Tram Website
https://edinburghtrams.com/

Edinburgh Airport Website
http://www.edinburghairport.com/transport-links
Edinburgh Airport Map
https://goo.gl/maps/HXhxRjEkWMs
Phone:0844 448 8833

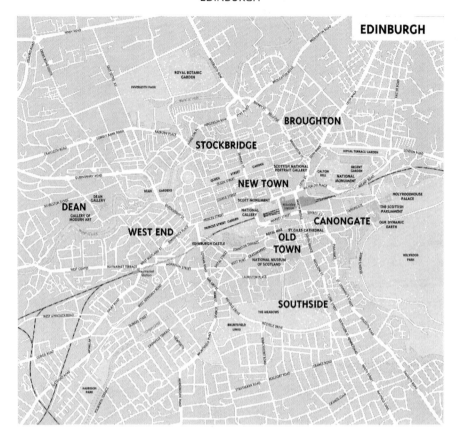

Buses –

This is the main form of transportation around the city. There are two major bus companies that operate in Edinburgh with a few smaller ones with fewer buses, but the main ones are the Lothian and First Bus. The latter has mostly buses that operate to and from outlying towns. So most of the buses you will see around the city are the dark red and white Lothian ones.

For convenience, you can purchase a Lothian Day Ticket for £4.00(£2.00 for kids) so you don't have to worry about getting the right change every single time. However, it is important to remember that you can only use these tickets on Lothian buses and not on the ones operated by other companies. If you plan to stay longer, then there are also other bus card options, such as the "Ridacard" and rechargeable "Citysmart" card.

Phone:0131 200 2323
Bus Website
http://edinburgh.cdmf.info/public/bus/list.htm

<u>Trains –</u>
Getting across the city by train is the fastest and most efficient way to do it. However, with most of the top attractions close to each other around the city center, trains are not the best way to see everything that the place offers. There are five main lines in the city with all trains

stopping at Waverly and Haymarket.

Phone:0344 811 0141
Train Website
https://www.scotrail.co.uk/scotland-by-rail
/scotlands-seven-cities/edinburgh

If you are traveling to Edinburgh from London, you can take a train from Kings Cross station in London to Edinburgh.The journey is about four and a half hours.

London to Edinburgh Train Website
https://www.virgintrainseastcoast.com/
our-destinations/trains-to-edinburgh/
London to Edinburgh Train Website 2
https://www.thetrainline.com/train-times/
london-to-edinburgh-waverley
London to Edinburgh Train Map
https://goo.gl/maps/2HvFU2YmceC2
Kings Cross Station London Map
https://goo.gl/maps/2Dww8nVm2DT2

<u>Car –</u>

Armed with a map of the city or perhaps an app on your smartphone that can give you accurate directions on how to get to your destination, traveling by car may seem to be the perfect way to see the capital. However, with the city constantly in a hustle and bustle, finding a place to park may be an adventure on its own. To address this, the city has set up multi-level car parks where you can leave your cars and tour by bus instead.

Cycle −

If you want to see the city on two wheels, then the great news is that Edinburgh has cycle paths to make this possible. Safely segregated from the main traffic thoroughfare, the city's extensive network of paths makes cycling a great and green way to tour the Scottish capital.

Address:276 Leith Walk, Edinburgh
Phone:0131 467 7775
Cycle Rent Website
http://www.leithcycleco.com/hire
Cycle Rent Map
https://goo.gl/maps/d2Nunce5AaM2

7

Famous Landmarks that you should not Miss

With two UNESCO World Heritage sites to offer plus dozens of other top attractions, Edinburgh is certainly a paradise for tourists. Hailed as the 'Athens of the North", it boasts of scenic and historical landmarks that draw tourists from all over the world. Below are the top attractions that visitors to the lovely city should not miss.

Edinburgh Castle

This impressive Scottish landmark is perched atop of Castle Rock and has towered over the city since the 13th century. Undoubtedly, the castle is the country's most popular tourist attraction with over a million visitors per year. Its location on the peak means one can get a spectacular view of the city's other famous spots like Princes Street, the Royal Mile and the Palace of Holyroodhouse.

The landmark also offers a feature that every tourist looks for in a castle. The entrance is through a drawbridge over an old moat with bronze statues of Scottish heroes William Wallace and Robert the Bruce welcoming you as you enter.

Edinburgh Castle serves as the majestic backdrop to the Edinburgh Military Tattoo, which takes place every summer as part of the Edinburgh Festival.

Address:Castlehill, Edinburgh
Phone:0131 225 9846
Edinburgh Castle Website
http://www.edinburghcastle.gov.uk/
Edinburgh Castle Map
https://goo.gl/maps/4Nayp1mvmcr

The castle is also known for the following:

The One O'clock Salute –
Located inside the castle is a distinctive curve walled section called the Half Moon Battery. On this wall is a time cannon, which is fired at

1pm from Monday to Friday.

What makes this tradition even more interesting is that while the cannon is being fired in the castle, a time ball is dropped at the Calton Hill Nelson Monument.

The Royal Palace – The palace was a witness to Scotland's colorful monarchy. In 1556, the ill-fated Mary, Queen of Scots, gave birth to the future King of England, James VI. The young prince assumed the Scottish throne on his first birthday and united England and Scotland in 1603. The last sovereign that stayed in the Royal Palace was Charles I when he spent the night there before his Scottish coronation in 1663.

Other attractions in the palace include The Great Hall, The Crown Jewels and the Stone of Destiny.

The Stone of Destiny is an ancient Scottish Monarchy symbol, which witnessed the coronations of Kings for centuries. The origin of the stone is wrapped in mystery, with the most famous legend being that it had been used by Jacob as a pillow when he dreamt of Jacob's ladder.

The Stone of Destiny used to be part of the King's throne in England until it was brought to Scotland in 1950. Nowadays, it sits in the throne room in the Royal Palace where you and other tourists can view it. The stone will leave Scotland again on the next coronation in Westminster Abbey.

St. Margaret's Chapel –

This private chapel, which used to be only for the Royals, is the oldest building in Edinburgh. It was built in the 11th century by David I and was dedicated to his mother, Queen Margaret, who was later canonized due to her many acts of charity. One interesting thing about the chapel is that it is maintained by the St. Margaret's Chapel Guild whose members are all named Margaret living in Scotland.

St. Margaret's Chapel Website
http://stmargaretschapel.com/
St. Margaret's Chapel Map
https://goo.gl/maps/b4Z8shDmjv82

The Palace of Holyroodhouse and Holyrood Abbey

The Palace of Holyroodhouse is the Queen's royal residence when she is in Scotland, which draws thousands of visitors all year round. The Monarch stays at the palace during Holyrood Week, which is usually at the end of June towards the beginning of July. And just like when she is in London, the Royal Standard of the United Kingdom is flown. The only difference is that it is the Scottish version that is used. Visitors to Edinburgh at that time are treated to a traditional parade including the Presentation of the Keys of the city of Edinburgh.

The spectacular and elegant palace has been at the center of Scottish history for centuries. It was the place where the coronation of James V and Charles I were held. It was also where James II and James IV were married.

The palace is open to the public when the Queen is not in residence, so visitors can tour the majestic Historic Apartments where Mary, Queen of Scots used to live. Another popular tourist attraction is the Historic Apartments with all its elegant furnishings, plasterwork, and tapestries.

Address:Canongate, Edinburgh
Phone:+44 131 556 5100
The Palace of Holyroodhouse Website
https://www.royalcollection.org.uk/visit/
palaceofholyroodhouse/what-to-see-and-do/abbey-tour
The Palace of Holyroodhouse Map

https://goo.gl/maps/4BoyYkKwmqD2

Royal Mile

The Royal Mile is the road that links Edinburgh Castle and the Palace Of Holyroodhouse. It is lined with historical landmarks and enchanting townhouses. Every Edinburgh visitor should make this road as one of the first stops with all the great shops including the traditional kilt makers, restaurants, and inns. The tall buildings on the street called "lands" can be as tall as 15-stories. The Royal Mile has narrow alleys with hidden backyards weaving in and around the "lands".

Tourists troop to the Royal Mile to see top attractions, like Castle Hill which is located at the upper end of the road. Some places that get quite a few visitors are the Camera Obscura and Outlook Tower. Your visit to the Royal Mile is also not complete if you do not drop by at the Tollbooth, with the city's tallest church towers and Lady Stair's Close where you can find the Writer's Museum.

Royal Mile Map
https://goo.gl/maps/hgwjRQtJpSJ2

St. Giles Cathedral

Located on the Royal Mile right at the heart of the Old Town, Edinburgh's historic cathedral was consecrated in 1243.The church features remarkable medieval carvings and impressive stained glass windows, making it stand out from other religious landmarks in the city.

You can take a stroll around the church or join one of the guided tours that are available upon request. Admission is free, but you are invited to make a £3.00 donation per person. If you wish to capture the serene and beautiful surroundings, then you need to get permits for photography from the Information Desk.

This attraction is located close to the rail station and is also accessible by bus.

Address:High St, Edinburgh

Phone:0131 225 9442

St. Giles Cathedral Website

http://www.stgilescathedral.org.uk/

St. Giles Cathedral Map

https://goo.gl/maps/DEguLktoSa22

Princes Street

Located in one of the two UNESCO World Heritage sites, New Town, Princes Street is almost a mile long with enchanting gardens and sophisticated shops. A walk down this busy place will bring you to

Jenners of Edinburgh, the oldest department store in the world. Other attractions that you can drop by include the grand House of Frasers on the western side and the quaint Princes Mall with its cozy shops and charming fountains.

While Princes Street is a shopper's paradise, it does have a lot more to offer. New Register House, the home of the Scottish National Archives is also an interesting place to visit. If you are interested in genealogy, then you will certainly have a grand time exploring the records on exhibit that go as far back as the 13th century.

One other place you should not miss visiting is the Princes Street Gardens, which is the home of the world's oldest floral clock. Visiting the gardens during winter is also a wonderful idea as you can spend an afternoon skating on the traditional outdoor rink.

Princes Street Website
http://www.princes-street.com/
Princes Street Map
https://goo.gl/maps/VkRaBLgUhD92

Calton Hill
One of the seven hills the city is said to be built on, this attraction offers a unique and breathtaking view of the city that local and foreign tourists should definitely not miss. You can admire the majestic Edinburgh Castle and bustling Princes Street on the west and treat your eyes to the Old town on the South side. With its impressive altitude, you can even see as far as the docks at Leith from the peak of Calton Hill.

Also, not to be missed attractions on the Hill are the National Monument and Nelson Monument. The former was erected as a memorial to the casualties of the Napoleonic Wars. The memorial was designed after Parthenon in Athens, but was unfortunately unfinished due to lack of funding.

The Nelson Monument, which was unveiled in 1816, is where the cannonball is dropped at the same time the 1pm canon is fired at Edinburgh Castle.

Calton Hill Map
https://goo.gl/maps/TCHsafkdkqJ2

8

The Art Scene: Museums and Galleries to See

The Museum of Childhood

Located at the Royal Mile, this museum is a favorite among kids of all ages. It is the first museum, which is dedicated to displaying exhibits on the history of childhood. Its unique exhibits include games and toys, clothing, club memorabilia and other topics that cover the different generations and various stages of childhood.

A visit to the museum is more than just a day spent reminiscing your childhood days, as it also serves as an educational experience that you and your kids can share. From Barbie Dolls to pedal cars, the exhibits feature everything that brings you back to the innocent days of fun and play.

The Museum of Childhood is open seven days a week, and admission is free. Of course, donations are welcome to help with the upkeep of the museum. While it does not have its own café or restaurant, it is located right at the heart of The Royal Mile, and so it is close to a lot of exciting places for meals and refreshments.

Address:42 High St, Royal Mile, Edinburgh
Phone:0131 529 4142
The Museum of Childhood Website
http://www.edinburghmuseums.org.uk/
Venues/Museum-of-Childhood
The Museum of Childhood Map
https://goo.gl/maps/rZBZCGPaD5R2

Museum of Edinburgh

Located on Huntly House on the historic Royal Mile, the Museum of Edinburgh features exhibits that show the city's history and origin. From the medieval period to present day, the museum's collections are divided into two main categories – the Decorative and History. The Decorative collections include immaculate silver, creative pottery, and stunning Scottish glass.

The History part of the exhibits has archeological collections and ones that show the evolution of life in Edinburgh. From things found at home to popular past times of different generations, the Museum of Edinburgh has the most interesting items on display.

The museum is open from Mondays to Saturdays. During the month of August, it is also open on Sundays. Admission is free with voluntary donations encouraged.

Address:142-146 Canongate, Edinburgh
Phone:0131 529 4143
Museum of Edinburgh Website
http://www.edinburghmuseums.org.uk/Venues/
Museum-of-Edinburgh.aspx
Museum of Edinburgh Map
https://goo.gl/maps/XPzgt1VF5qm

Travelling Gallery

This unique art experience is a self-contained and mobile exhibit, which began in 1978. The first show was held in a double-decker that had been converted for the exhibit. The shows in the following years were so successful that by 1983, a custom built vehicle had been commissioned.

The Travelling Gallery features two shows a year, with each one running for an average of four months. It brings the exhibits closer to the public by staging it at different venues every day. It is something, which is certainly worth checking out when you are in the Scottish capital.

Because the gallery is mobile, it is highly recommended to contact the team in charge to find out where the show will be for the day you wish to go. Admission is free, so it is an adventure, which is culturally enriching without breaking your holiday budget.

Phone:0131 529 3930
e-mail: travellinggallery@edinburgh.gov.uk
Travelling Gallery Website
http://www.travellinggallery.com/

The Writer's Museum

Located in the Lady Stair's House on the Royal Mile, the Writer's Museum celebrates the three biggest names in Scottish literature. On the doorway at the entrance to the museum are words of warning that say "Fear the Lord and depart from evil", creating a mysterious air.

The three Scottish greats featured in the museum are Robert Burns, Sir Walter Scott, and Robert Louis Stevenson. Exhibits include portraits of Burns, the poet who wrote "Auld Lang Syne", personal items of Stevenson, the man responsible for novels such as Treasure Island,

Kidnapped and the Curious Case of Dr. Jekyll and Mr. Hyde, and the printing press where Scott's famous Waverly novels were printed on.

Scott is also known for his other works Ivanhoe and The Lady and the Lake.

Visitors like yourself will also have a grand time at the museum shop where you can get literary souvenirs to help you remember your museum experience.

Address:Lady Stair's House, Lady Stair's Close, Lawnmarket, Edinburgh
Phone:0131 529 4901
The Writer's Museum Website
http://www.edinburghmuseums.org.uk/Venues/
The-Writers--Museum.aspx
The Writer's Museum Map
https://goo.gl/maps/68qdw5sUHSR2

City Art Center

Art lovers of all ages will have a spectacular time at this six level gallery located near the Waverly Station. It features traditional and contemporary Scottish and Foreign art. The museum holds rolling exhibits that include photography, architecture and even Roman and Egyptian artifacts.

One of the most interesting exhibits featured in the gallery that had sci-fi and comic con fans going crazy was one of the Star Wars costumes.

Admission to the permanent exhibits is free with donations encouraged. Temporary shows, however, have admission fees.

2 Market St, Edinburgh
Phone:0131 529 3993
City Art Center Website
http://www.edinburghmuseums.org.uk/Venues/
City-Art-Centre.aspx
City Art Center Map
https://goo.gl/maps/SS1hscb1exv

9

The Gastronomic Scene: Restaurants and Coffee Shops

Edinburgh is a gastronomic experience that any food lover will certainly enjoy. The Scottish capital has the most Michelin star restaurants in the country. You will find it absolutely delightful with different types of cuisine – from traditional Scottish to popular international favorites like pizza and burgers. Below are some of the restaurants and café's that locals and visitors recommend trying at least once.

Castle Terrace

The restaurant fuses local Scottish ingredients and elegant French style preparations. Castle Terrace is one of the most popular dining experiences in the city with reservations that you need to make months ahead. The good news is that you have a hundred percent assurance that the food and service will be worth the wait. You can be sure that the restaurant lives up to its reputation as a rising superstar in the culinary world. In fact, this Old Town treasure only took 15 months to earn its first Michelin star.

The a la carte menu is updated per season, so their customers can take full advantage of ingredients that are locally available. With scrumptious dishes that include mouthwatering starters, delectable entrees, and sinful desserts, you can make sure that it is an experience worth spending money on.

Castle Terrace is also known for its impressive wine selection, which compliments the dishes served in the gastronomic haven.

Phone:0131 229 1222
Email:info@castleterracerestaurant.com
Castle Terrace Website
https://castleterracerestaurant.com/
Castle Terrace Map
https://goo.gl/maps/FyQo2ekfEQk

Oink Grassmarket

Located in Old Town's amazing Victoria Street is Oink Grassmarket. It is a restaurant, which specializes in hog roasts that are a treat for the senses. Even before getting to the restaurant, you can already smell the inviting aroma of roast as it wafts down the street.

Oink Grassmarket was set up by two farmers who turned moreish pork roast into a culinary dream. Served in three different sizes, the pulled pork dishes come with fluffy morning rolls, crackling and your sides including haggis and sage and onion stuffing. Soup of the day and cold drinks are also served to complete the meal. It is a filling dining experience that does not break the bank, with prices ranging from £2.95 for the Piglet size to the Grunter at £4.95

Address:34 Victoria St, Old Town, Edinburgh
Phone:07771 968233
Oink Grassmarket Website
http://www.oinkhogroast.co.uk/
Oink Grassmarket Map
https://goo.gl/maps/X8rN9ccx3rw

The Witchery

This elegant restaurant offers the sophistication of fine dining without the uncomfortable, stiff environment. Located a stone's throw away from the Edinburg Castle, this Royal Mile treasure is nestled in a 16th-century building in the heart of Old Town. While it is a tad pricier than other restaurants, it does deliver the experience one expects from the amount you pay for.

It boasts an extensive wine list with around 800 selections, so you can find the perfect one to match your scrumptious meal. Patrons of this traditional restaurant recommend the lamb wellington for two or their signature steak tartare.

The prices while not cheap are still certainly affordable with a 3-course meal available at £36.00 and a 2-course lunch or theater supper for just £19.95

Address:Castlehill, The Royal Mile, Edinburgh
Phone:0131 225 5613
The Witchery Website
http://www.thewitchery.com/
The Witchery Map
https://goo.gl/maps/WsEqrqHMvaU2

Nobles café, Bar and Restaurant

This popular food haunt is located on the Leith shore close to the scenic walkways. With its unique menu of Scottish ingredients and seafood like Haddock and Chips and Moules Frites, you will certainly be treated to a gastronomically delightful meal. Nobles also offer an impressive selection of ale from the tap and bottled.

Address:44a Constitution St, Edinburgh
Phone:0131 629 7215
Nobles café, Bar and Restaurant Website
http://www.noblesbarleith.co.uk/
Nobles café, Bar and Restaurant Map
https://goo.gl/maps/DEgjPsG9QTr

First Coast

When on holiday in Edinburgh, the best places to eat are really the restaurants or bistros that locals frequent. With flavorful dishes at affordable prices, you get a taste of the city without breaking the bank. First Coast is certainly one of those places.

Located in Dalry Road, this award winning Bistro has been a neighborhood favorite for the past decade. With a diverse menu that includes tasty seafood, meat, and vegetarian dishes, customers are treated to a unique dining experience.

First Coast uses local ingredients and fuses it with international flavors, such as Asian and Italian to create an unforgettable meal. The bistro also offers specials that change regularly to keep everything new and interesting. Bestsellers include Thai marinated chicken salad with cucumber, pepper and mango and ox cheek, polenta, parsnips & gremolata.

Prices are also pretty affordable at the elegantly decorated bistro. Ala carte meals range from £4.00 starters to £19.00 Angus Steak Entrée. You will also love the wine selections offered.

Address:97-101 Dalry Rd, Edinburgh
Phone:0131 313 4404
First Coast Website
http://www.first-coast.co.uk/
First Coast Map
https://goo.gl/maps/LWZvgrspkb52

10

Edinburg Night Life

Edinburgh, at night, is certainly as exciting and as adventurous as the unique attractions it offers. With the reputation as being the UK city with the most number of bars per capita, you are sure to find one, which is right up your alley. Here are a few recommended places to hang out in to have a memorable night.

Hector's

This charming and inviting place is everything you have ever imag-
ined a Scottish Pub to be. With a relaxed ambiance and great ale that
include local brews to international selections, Hector's is a local and
tourist favorite. You can relax and enjoy a bit of conversation with the
other patrons as you enjoy a relaxing Sunday evening sipping on beer
or Bloody Marys and snacking on some delectable roasts.

Address:47-49 Deanhaugh St, Edinburgh
Phone:0131 343 1735
Hector's Website
http://www.hectorsstockbridge.co.uk/
Hector's Map
https://goo.gl/maps/cTKHTPH2CuA2

The Bongo Club

For some dancing and a night of music, the Bongo Club is one of
the best places to head to. While it has been around for years, it
used to have a nomadic life as it moved from venue to venue. The
reason behind this was that there were no areas established as the
best nightclub scene. However, in 2013, it found a permanent home.
Now, it is literally an underground scene, located beneath the Central
Library.

The club has become a popular place to unwind and let loose to the
different types of music from reggae to soul that it offers. A quick visit
to its website can fill you in on the events that will be happening, so
you can check what is on during your stay in Edinburgh.

Address:66 Cowgate, Edinburgh
Phone:0131 558 8844

The Bongo Club Website
http://www.thebongoclub.co.uk/
The Bongo Club Map
https://goo.gl/maps/4UcwA9mQADF2

Sneaky Pete's

Located in Edinburgh's nightclub area at Cowgate, this 100-capacity club has featured gigs from up and coming as well as famous artists to promote the local music scene. The décor is street influenced with graffiti and murals adorning the seemingly dirty walls and dance floor; the club has a grungy ambiance that appeals to its patrons. If you are looking for some underground music and an evening spent experiencing Edinburgh's nightlife, then a visit to Sneaky Pete's is a must.

Be ready to dance and jam the night away with dozens of others on a crowded and vibrant dance floor. It is an evening that you will definitely not forget for a long time.

Address:73 Cowgate, Edinburgh
Phone:0131 225 1757
Sneaky Pete's Website
http://www.sneakypetes.co.uk/
Sneaky Pete's Map
https://goo.gl/maps/TZbmShHApdM2

The Sheep Heid Inn

This historic pub located at the Causeway in Duddingston has been a favorite not just by the locals but by poets and past monarchs as well. Enchantingly restored, the Sheep Heid Inn is the oldest surviving watering hole in Edinburgh.

Nowadays, the pub's customers are mostly climbers or hikers of Arthur's Seat who are looking for a place to rest and relax before or after a strenuous day. The popular pub offers a taste of the country while still being in the city. The gastropub also offers a delectable treat to its hungry patrons.

Some of the foods included in the menu are BBQ Shredded Pork Sandwiches and Sausages and Mash. Prices are also reasonable with meals averaging about £8.00. The pub also has mid-week price specials, like a 3-course dinner with a bottle of wine included for only £22.00

Address:43-45 The Causeway, Edinburgh
Phone:0131 661 7974
The Sheep Heid Inn Website
http://www.thesheepheidedinburgh.co.uk/
The Sheep Heid Inn Map
https://goo.gl/maps/YHxk2yAHQ6z

The Electric Circus

Aptly named, this club can be practically anything one needs it to be. It is a part gig venue, part karaoke bar and part club. Located right behind the Waverly station, this incredible chameleon of a club has been the site for numerous colorful events, from up and coming bands showcasing their fresh music to hopefuls and wannabe's belting out to a chosen karaoke tune.

Patrons dance until the wee hours of the morning, celebrating the eccentric ambiance of the spot that has certainly and most definitely earned its name, circus.

You and your friends can immerse yourself in retro music, sing along with everybody as the red ball bounces across the screen or participate in fun workshops or classes like burlesque dance classes held in one of the rooms in the circus.

Address:36-39 Market St, Edinburgh
Phone:0131 226 4224
The Electric Circus Website
http://www.theelectriccircus.biz/
The Electric Circus Map
https://goo.gl/maps/Q76AotdFyaE2

11

The Whisky Experience

There is one thing that you certainly cannot miss out on when you are in Edinburgh. You can't expect it to be a complete Scottish holiday unless you have some liquid gold or also more popularly known as Whisky. The best way to describe this drink is basically, Scotland in a glass. The Gaelic word for whiskey describes exactly how important it is to the locals.

Whisky, in Gaelic, is "uisge beatha", which means "the water of life", so make sure to enjoy a tour of any of the distilleries in and around the city. The best way to get started is to head off to the Scotch Whisky Experience on the Royal Mile.

The Scotch Whisky Experience has been introducing enthusiasts and beginners to the wonderful world of Scotch. It offers 1-day training school, enjoyable tastings and exciting tours.

In the training school, you spend the entire day learning about whiskey. Most attendees are from the hospitality industry working to get certified. The course includes entertaining and educational hands-on activities, where you can even learn how to make your own drink at home. At the end of the session, you will get a certificate of expertise as proof that you had completed the course.

The next part of the experience is to book one of the available tours where you can explore nearby distilleries. These tours often include scotch tasting to help you better appreciate this Scottish traditional drink. The tour prices vary, ranging from £14.50 to £65.00 depending on what is included in the package.

There are also other Whisky tours that you can join that start in the city and lasts for a few days, continuing to the whiskey region of Scotland.

Address:354 Castlehill, Edinburgh
Phone:0131 220 0441
The Scotch Whisky Experience Website
https://www.scotchwhiskyexperience.co.uk/
The Scotch Whisky Experience Map
https://goo.gl/maps/QJzDhMMTjWx

12

Only in Edinburgh: What you can Only Experience in the Scottish Capital

The Scots have always been proud and unique people and these local customs, traditions and specialties are best examples of just how amazingly different the city of Edinburgh is.

The Tartan Weaving Company

While it is common knowledge that the skirt looking clothing worn my Scotsmen are called kilt, not many people know about the material that is used for it. Some people mistakenly call it plaid, but the proper term is tartan. During your visit to Edinburgh, you will find no shortage of this material. While most of the ones for sale are of poor quality and created more for tourists, there is a place where you can head off to and get good tartan material.

Located at the end of the Royal Mile and just before the Castle Esplanade is a non-descript building, which houses some of the best kilt material in Edinburgh. It is called the Tartan Weaving Company. It is the perfect place to get your material for some serious kilting and learn about how the material is made. The company offers displays of the history of tartan making, as well as tours of the factory to give visitors a glimpse of the process.

The Tartan Weaving Company Website
http://www.heritageofscotland.com/
The Tartan Weaving Company Map
https://goo.gl/maps/wSupnVsp45m

Unique Cuisine

If you have ever watched movies or documentaries about Scotland, then there is a great chance that you already come across some of the unique food offerings it has. While quite interesting, some of these may need an acquired taste to fully enjoy, but as they say, when in Rome! So, it would certainly be a pity if you do not give a couple of these at least one try.

Haggis and Neeps – Traditionally served on Burns Night, this national dish has become famous worldwide because of the interesting assortment of filling that goes into the sausage. Haggis is made of innards and offal chopped up lungs, heart, and liver mixed with onions, suet, herbs and spices.

The filling is mixed together and stuffed into a skin bag made of a sheep's stomach. It is usually served with mashed potatoes and topped with a rich whisky sauce. While it may not sound appetizing, it does have an interesting taste and texture. Be sure to give it a try during your holiday at Edinburgh.

Address:Paisley Close, 105 High St, Edinburgh
Phone:0131 225 7064
The Royal McGregor Website (Hagis)
http://www.royalmcgregor.co.uk/

The Royal McGregor Map
https://goo.gl/maps/MHrqfvaP5CR2

Powsowdie – When called this, tasting the broth does not seem quite so adventurous. However, once you find out what it is also known as then it may seem like quite a daring task. Powsowdie is commonly known as Sheep's Head Broth. And yes, it really is made from sheep's head. The preparation may make some people cringe, but it is really quite rich and flavorful.

Rowan Jelly – While Jelly may not seem unique, this one is different from most fruit jellies that are either sweet or tart. Rowan berries are slightly bitter, making it a popular accompaniment to game or other rich tasting dish.

Scottish National Drink –

Edinburgh as the Scottish capital is a representation of Scotland's traditions and customs. One popular tradition is the country's national drink which is Whisky. As already discussed, there are quite a few distilleries around Edinburgh which is the reason why Whisky tours have become popular.

Address:197 High St, Edinburgh
Phone:+44 131 220 5277
The Albanach Website (Whiskey Bar)
http://www.albanach-edinburgh.co.uk/menu
The Albanach Map
https://goo.gl/maps/HpEFh6qsjtA2

Now, the unofficial national drink of Scotland is a carbonated beverage known as Irn Bru or Iron Brew. The bright orange colored drink has clever marketing techniques, which is the reason why it continues to rank over other internationally popular brands like Coca-Cola and Pepsi. It is a soft drink that you may want to give a try before leaving Edinburgh so you can experience exactly why locals love it so much.

13

Staying Safe While on Holiday

While the Scots are known to be warm and friendly, it is still wise to be aware of the best ways to stay safe while on holiday in Edinburgh. Here are some tips to keep in mind while you are in the safest city in the UK.

Take note of Emergency Numbers that you may need, such as local hospitals and police stations. The Emergency hotline in Edinburgh is **999**.

Some of the top attractions in Edinburgh are located in hilly areas. Wear comfortable shoes to prevent any accidents while walking around the city. In addition, be sure to bring necessities such as bottles of water, jackets, sunscreen and any other season appropriate things. The weather may get dry and warm or chilly on certain days, make sure you are prepared to deal with these conditions.

Watch out for tourist traps. Edinburgh is a popular tourist destination that draws people from all over the world. With so many folks coming to town, the tourist trade is certainly on the up and up. So be careful when shopping for souvenirs as most of these may be overpriced and not of good quality.

If you are planning to take the bus around the city, make sure you have plenty of change to avoid any inconvenience. Bus drivers will rarely split your money if you do not have the exact amount so you may end up losing money over bus rides. You can also opt to get the day tickets so you no longer have to worry about getting the right change when getting on the buses.

Check up with local law enforcement or tourism offices about the places to avoid. While Edinburgh is generally a safe city to explore, tourists are advised to stay away from the Wester Hailes in the southwest and the housing estates of Pilton and Muirhouse as these areas are known to have a high crime rate and drug abuse.

Scotland Police Website
http://www.scotland.police.uk/contact-us/

Emergency Number - 999

14

Recommended 3-day Travel Itinerary

With so much to offer, it seems almost impossible to fit in all the sites and sounds that Edinburgh has to offer in just 72 hours. However, with the right plan, you can fully experience the city in three days whatever time of the year you go. Below is a recommended travel itinerary for you and your family.

However, before we start on the different landmarks and attractions you can visit, the first step is to find a centrally located place to stay. The great news is that as discussed in a previous chapter, there are various types of accommodations in and around the city center that will surely fit your budget. If you are traveling with family or friends, you can choose a serviced apartment or boutique hotel to stretch your budget.

Day 1 – Edinburgh Castle, Royal Mile and the Palace of Holyroodhouse

You can spend your first day exploring the most popular attractions of Edinburgh. Edinburgh Castle and Holyroodhouse are connected by the Royal Mile, so you can explore it without the need to travel in circles.

Start with the majestic Edinburgh Castle at Castle Rock Hill and explore the fort that started it all. Aside from the different sites inside the castle like the Royal Palace and St. Margaret's Chapel, you can also enjoy your first bird's eye view of the city.

Edinburgh Castle Map
https://goo.gl/maps/WebxjMmkoXN2

After getting a fill of the Castle, you can head on to the Royal Mile and immerse in the beautiful buildings and picturesque winding alleys. The road is lined with charming cafes and stores that offer a taste of the Scottish capital. The Royal Mile is also home to quite a few interesting museums that you may want to pop into and explore. Most of these do not charge an admission fee and only ask for minimal donations.

Royal Mile Map
https://goo.gl/maps/9C4ZXNDSUQK2

Just a few minutes down the road is the Queen's official residence in Scotland, the Palace of Holyroodhouse. If you are in town around the end of June, then you can get a glimpse of the Scottish version of the Royal Standard being flown.

Holyroodhouse Map
https://goo.gl/maps/RKF4JF2MiAT2

The Palace has sections that you can tour, so be sure to sign up for that so you can see the elegant furnishings and beautiful works of art on display.

Day 2 – New Town and Leith

After a hearty and filling Scottish breakfast, your second day will be, once again, a treat for all senses. Spend the day exploring the sites of New Town. The area is full of shops where you can start filling up on souvenirs to remember your trip by. Whether you choose a tartan or some other colorful and clever knickknack, have fun exploring what the stores have to offer.

Word Of Mouth Website (Breakfast Recommendation)
https://www.facebook.com/Word-of-Mouth

-Cafe-2276361163937635/
Word Of Mouth Map
https://goo.gl/maps/YbcMxbw5u5u
Address:3A Albert St, Edinburgh
Phone:+44 131 554 4344

Princes Street in New Town also has a lot of gastronomical delights, so you can take a quick break for lunch while also admiring the beautiful parks in the area. Before leaving the street, make sure to head to the Gardens and take loads of pictures for your Instagram and other social media accounts.

Princes Street Map
https://goo.gl/maps/n2zTk9FL9Lq

Afterward, you can go to Leith where you can stop by the Royal Yacht Brittania. This floating museum is ranked as the 3rd must see attractions in Edinburgh. This historical Royal floating palace is a treat to explore. With rooms and decks included in the audio guided tour, you and the rest of your group can have a glimpse of the Royal Family's official yacht.

Address:Ocean Terminal, Ocean Dr, Edinburgh
Phone:0131 555 5566
Royal Yacht Brittania Website
http://www.royalyachtbritannia.co.uk/
Royal Yacht Brittania Map
https://goo.gl/maps/22hpFGyjtWJ2

If you want to do some more shopping then you can have your fill at the Ocean Terminal, or you can simply relax in one of the many cafes and restaurants inside the shopping complex to recharge before your next adventure.

While you are in Leith, be sure to take a leisure stroll down the paths of the Water of Leith Walkway. If you have bicycles rented for the day, it also makes for a good biking path. The area is an interesting palette of colors with the water and surrounding foliage.

Water of Leith Walkway Website
http://www.waterofleith.org.uk/walkway
Water of Leith Walkway Map
https://goo.gl/maps/m4ttpjL8BRm

Day 3 – Calton Hill, Arthur's Seat and the Roslyn Chapel

Your last day in the city is by no means any different from the previous days. It is still full of adventure and excitement as you continue to explore what the city has to offer.

If you want a bird's eye view of the city on your final day, you can choose between Arthur's Seat and Calton Hill. While both are spectacular locations, the former is a bit more strenuous. Pick which of those two peaks will fit your hiking skills.

Arthur's Seat Map

https://goo.gl/maps/2wR9wyvUK762
Calton Hill Map
https://goo.gl/maps/bTKjHy9Yk4r

There are also still quite a few galleries, museums, parks and castles that you can explore, so simply pick out the ones that capture your interest, as well as the rest of your party. The bus lines in the city are dependable so you should have no problem getting about. Check out the Writer's Museum to learn more about the greatest Scottish writers responsible for literary works such as Dr. Jekyll and Mr. Hyde.

Writer's Museum Map
https://goo.gl/maps/GaXgAASg2FR2

You can visit the Museum of Childhood to view interesting exhibits that feature items from the different stages of growing up. From doll houses to spinning tops, it is a great way to reminisce about your childhood and learn about previous generations.

Museum of Childhood Map
https://goo.gl/maps/8erwpEZDG342

One destination that you cannot leave without seeing, especially if you are a Dan Brown fan is the Roslyn Chapel. This chapel was made famous in the novel "The Da Vinci Code". As a result, it has drawn more and more visitors to this unique church, which combines different architectural elements.

Roslyn Chapel Map
https://goo.gl/maps/6RigguRARBv
Roslyn Chapel Website
http://www.rosslynchapel.com/
Address:Chapel Loan, Roslin
Phone:+44 131 440 2159

15

Conclusion

Whether you are traveling with friends or family, Edinburgh has a lot to offer. With its numerous historical landmarks, picturesque views and exciting festivals that are happening almost the whole year round, it is no surprise that it continues to attract tourists from all over the world.

A city that fuses busy urban lifestyle with the laidback and relaxed ambiance of country living, Edinburgh is an ideal spot for whatever holiday you may have in mind.

From romantic getaways to adventures with friends and family, you can be sure that you will find something to satisfy your senses in the Scottish capital.

Thank you again for downloading the book! I hope you were able to get the information you need to enjoy your trip to Edinburgh.

If you received value from this book, I want to ask you for a favour.Would you be kind enough to leave a review for this book on Amazon?

This document is geared towards providing exact and reliable information in regards to the topic and issue covered. The publication is sold with the idea that the publisher is not required to render accounting, officially permitted, or otherwise, qualified services. If advice is necessary, legal or professional, a practiced individual in the profession should be ordered.

– From a Declaration of Principles which was accepted and approved equally by a Committee of the American Bar Association and a Committee of Publishers and Associations.

The information provided herein is stated to be truthful and consistent, in that any liability, in terms of inattention or otherwise, by any usage or abuse of any policies, processes, or directions contained within is the solitary and utter responsibility of the recipient reader. Under no circumstances will any legal responsibility or blame be held against the publisher for any reparation, damages, or monetary loss due to the information herein, either directly or indirectly.

Respective authors own all copyrights not held by the publisher.

The information herein is offered for informational purposes solely, and is universal as so. The presentation of the information is without contract or any type of guarantee assurance.

The trademarks that are used are without any consent, and the publication of the trademark is without permission or backing by the trademark owner. All trademarks and brands within this book are for clarifying purposes only and are the owned by the owners themselves, not affiliated with this document.

Made in the USA
Columbia, SC
23 February 2025

54307740R00052